WILLINGLY WOULD I BURN

WILLINGLY WOULD I BURN

LAURA LEHEW

MoonPath Press

Copyright © 2013 Laura LeHew
all rights reserved

Poetry
ISBN 978-1-936657-08-7

Cover art "Universal Phoenix"
by Mitchell Davidson Bentley
AtomicFlyStudios.com

Design by Tonya Namura
using Minion Pro

MoonPath Press is dedicated to publishing the best poets of the U.S. Northwest Pacific states

MoonPath Press
PO Box 445
Tillamook, OR 97141

MoonPathPress@gmail.com

http://MoonPathPress.com

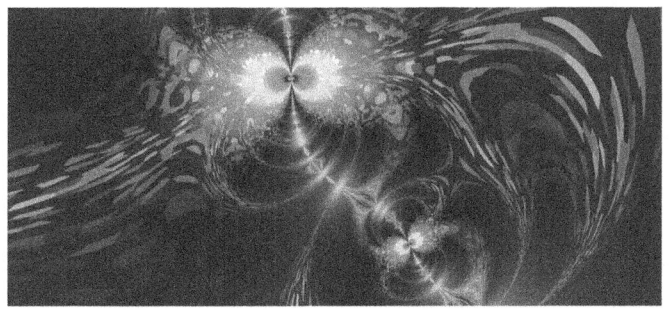

This book is dedicated to N^2—
gone but not forgotten.

CONTENTS

- 3   MAYBE NOW I CAN WRITE SOMETHING BESIDES CODE
- 4   MEANWHILE
- 5   A WORD PROBLEM
- 7   I THOUGHT YOU WERE IN MENSA
- 8   FOUR
- 9   A WORD PROBLEM, 2
- 11   A WORD PROBLEM, 3
- 13   IF YOU HAVE A DAUGHTER— TEACH HER TO FLY
- 14   ADJACENT ANGLES
- 15   A WORD PROBLEM, 4
- 17   THE POEM THAT CAN'T BE WRITTEN
- 18   MOSQUITO
- 19   THE BIRD FLU
- 21   A WORD PROBLEM, 5
- 22   THE NEW MATH
- 24   A WORD PROBLEM, 6
- 25   THE TENSION OF TRIANGULATION
- 26   FRACTIONS
- 27   WHY AREN'T THERE MORE WOMEN (aka GIRLS) IN MATH AND SCIENCE?
- 30   YOU HAVE MALE
- 32   STANDARDIZED TESTING
- 38   SHOULD WE VANISH
- 40   STILL LIFE AS MIXED MEDIA
- 41   THE L5 SOCIETY
- 42   THE EFFECT OF EVIDENCE IN CONVINCING THE MIND

- 43 LOGOMACHY
- 44 MAKING SENSE OF INVESTING
- 46 SOME LIMITS TO HAPPINESS
- 47 THE DEMOGRAPHICS OF PRISON
- 48 UNCONTESTED AIRSPACE
- 49 A COMPREHENSIVE RELATIVISTIC THEORY ALTERNATIVE TO THE DARK MATTER PARADIGM
- 50 THE PARAMETER OF REGRET
- 52 ALL OF MY ALTERNATIVE ROUTES HAVE ALTERNATIVE ROUTES

- 53 ACKNOWLEDGMENTS
- 55 NOTES
- 56 ABOUT THE AUTHOR

In mathematics the art of proposing a question must be held of higher value than solving it.

—Georg Cantor

WILLINGLY WOULD I BURN

MAYBE NOW I CAN WRITE SOMETHING BESIDES CODE

start again with the obvious
time is luck
if only the light was here and

dreams—
probability like gravity
the odds catching up

I've made mistakes
gathered the pale
sediment of our lives

raven and dove
harbingers of hope
tell us everything

a murder of silence
echoes of the larger truth
the path between us slippery

I bring change—the fallacy
finger to flame, a fear
of apologizing

using phantom digits to solve
mathematical problems and all
the algorithms it would take

MEANWHILE
after Wislawa Szymborska

One out of eight will. Someday.
Younger. Older.
It may develop.
It has developed.
It developed—but not in you.

You were not the one because you are still young.
Because no mother, no daughter, no sister developed it.
Because you never had it. Because your weight is normal.
Because you don't drink much. Because you had a child.
Because you had a child before you turned thirty.
Because you are a male.

Fortunate you had your period after you were twelve.
Menopause before fifty-five, normal genes, a good diet,
a non-smoker, mindful meditation.
For those fortunate monthly self-examinations.

What would happen if you were the
twelve point five percent of the population,
the one out of eight?

Where does the math begin? Acquaintances,
second cousins twice removed, check-out clerks, drive thru
tellers, dental hygienists, that woman at the dog park?
Are they a part of your count?

A myriad of technicalities—
juxtapose your heart:
You? Me?

A WORD PROBLEM

Four daughters race around me in opposite directions, at a constant rate. They start at the same point and meet every 30 seconds. If they move in the same direction, they meet every 120 seconds. They stay in St. Luke's seven thousand two hundred minutes; approximately long enough for closure. If a standard vinyl covered innerspring mattress for a hospital bed is 36" x 80", what is on the mind of each daughter?

Hints:

1) Let w = the rate of daughter 1
   Let x = the rate of daughter 2
   Let y = the rate of daughter 3
   Let z = the rate of daughter 4
   Let a = the rate of the missing son

2) Use substitution or elimination

Answer (round each answer individually):

   Solve for daughter 1: (1)≠(2)
   Divert unwanted questions, attempt conversion

   Solve for daughter 2: (2)≠(3)
   Substitute for a thinner daughter

   Solve for daughter 3: (3)≠(4)
   Substitute for a smarter daughter

   Solve for daughter 4: (4)≠(a)
   Substitute for chicken fingers and a loaf of bread

Solve for missing son: $(a) \neq (1)$
Substitute for a new family (see daughters x, y, and z)

I am in a hospital headed toward home hospice. Its route is circular.

I THOUGHT YOU WERE IN MENSA
waltz wave

> "Poetry is finer and more philosophical than history; for poetry expresses the universal, and history only the particular."
> —Aristotle

Yet
accuse
me
of not
being a
writer;
a
poet's
charge? Nothing
less than witness:
injustice
oil spills
rapes
vagrants
wars
money
greed
justice
love.

FOUR

the number of completion/the number of death
the cross and the square
the total of the created and the revealed = all
    that perishes
cardinal points, winds, columns of the universe,
    elements, seasons, humors

every quarter hour she queries *is it 4 yet—*
then, *could I have 4 cigarettes*
look 4 crows, look 4 crows, look
4 crows, look look look look

remember when dad forgot everything
forgot what he was ordering
      dad's dead, you remember
sure, yeah, sure but do you remember when dad forgot

he actually
                    forgot
      everything
                          e v e r y t h i n g

A WORD PROBLEM, 2

Thirty years ago your sister married her high school boyfriend. They have two children. One is disabled, the other is unmarried with three children under the age of five. Five years ago your sister and brother-in-law paid off their first home; their mortgage was $50,000. That year your brother-in-law went on strike at his union job for unfair management practices. He'd been with the company over twenty years. He was fired. He couldn't afford an attorney to fight the union. He took a job doing construction as a contractor. Four years ago they bought their dream home; their new mortgage payment is $1,200.00 a month for thirty years. The house has a pool. Two years ago your brother-inlaw suffered some health issues and wasn't able to work. He had no benefits. He was a hard worker and he didn't lose his job. He wasn't paid while he was in the hospital. He wasn't paid while he was rehabbing his injury. It was job related. Six months ago your sister was laid off her job as an accounts payable clerk. Walked her out the door. She made $12.50 an hour plus benefits. She was due for a raise. Her COBRA is about to run out. Her daughter can't always afford water or electricity at her apartment and brings the three children to the house for baths on the weekend. Unemployment states your sister must take whatever job is offered to her.

If she is offered a job at the kennel, which job should she accept:

- a. kennel cleaner, dog walker, working across the bridge twenty miles away from 6 AM–2 PM for $7.25 an hour/plus benefits. Note: she would not have to pay for care for her disabled son since she could meet his bus at 3 PM

b. kennel cleaner ½ time and customer service ½ time, working > five miles away, from 6 AM–2 PM three days a week and 9 AM–5 PM two days a week for $7.25 an hour/plus benefits. Note: she would have to pay for care for her disabled son from 3 PM to 5:30 PM two days a week

c. lie to unemployment and take a class at the local community college, be out the cost of the class, gas, child care, look for and pay for reasonable health insurance in hopes of netting a job at a later date that will net her ≥ $12.50 an hour she made before she was laid off

The first rain of the season your brother-in-law slides into another car at a stop light. Factor in the cost of a new van.

A WORD PROBLEM, 3

Karyn, a serial monogamist, holds a doctoral degree in ministry. Every 30 days Karyn purchases 3 pounds of Peet's Gaia Organic Blend® coffee at $13.95/lb. for a cost of $41.85. Minus her Peetniks discount of $4.00. Plus $8.00 shipping which is calculated at time of shipment [Ground–Cont. U.S. (3–8 business days)]. There is no sales tax since Karyn lives in Oregon. Weekly she purchases a 32 oz. carton of RICE DREAM® Enriched Original Organic rice milk, the perfect non-dairy beverage, enriched with vitamins A, D & B12 with the same amount of calcium as milk. It is low fat and all natural and costs $3.70. She drives 2.55 miles to the grocery store.

The cost of gas is currently $3.23 a gallon. Karyn's 1999 periwinkle blue VW Passat with heated black leather seats gets 21 miles to the gallon in the city. It has 105,000 miles on the odometer. Recently Karyn went to the car dealer to have the oil changed, mentioning to the service rep that some lights had just come on. 5 hours later the technician informed her that the ABS system had failed, her coolant bottle was cracked and leaking, the cam adjustor and valve cover gaskets were leaking oil on the exhaust manifold and engine block and the motor mounts were leaking hydraulic dampening fluid. The tech suggested replacement. The power steering fluid was dark and dirty; it needed flushing. Brake fluids were due to be changed, the fuel system needed to be flushed and a fuel filter replaced. AC was not working as the system was reaching "high suck" pressures due to the AC fan having failed. They suggested replacement. Estimated cost of repairs: $3,200. Blue book value of the car, if it were in moderate shape: $3,208. The car dealer proposed a trade-in. She declined. Karyn did, however, authorize an oil change for $29.99 and paid $185.36 for the diagnosis including labor, parts and miscellaneous. It was the hottest day of the year, reaching 97°. Driving the car home with the windows down Karyn adjusted the mirrors. The knob broke off and flew out the window.

The Nissan Leaf, a 100% electric car with zero emissions, is priced under $35,000. (Less than the average driver spends on gas over 10 years). MSRP is $33,720 with federal tax savings from 0-$7,500. After tax savings, Karyn's net costs could be as low as $26,220, assuming $1,999 initial customer payment. Alternatively, Karyn could purchase a 1999 black Mercedes at the cost of $13,999. It has been converted to use bio-diesel and is available today.

16 oz. rice milk lattes with sugar free vanilla cost $4.25 from Full City Roasters. Full City is 7 miles away from Karyn's home. Which variant gives Karyn the smallest carbon footprint: buying her coffee out or brewing her own? Please show your work and don't forget to add in the cost of tipping the barista.

IF YOU HAVE A DAUGHTER—
TEACH HER TO FLY

bodies against the brink
accepting directives
a bruising shuffle

the torments of negative space
extractions—protocols—extermination
unchanging templates

veiled histories
amplifying identifying DNA sequences
proof of death isn't what it used to be

it's all so obvious
the larger truth

ADJACENT ANGLES

my mother never saw a Bloody Mary she wouldn't drink
never had an orgasm until I told her how
never loved my father

at his funeral a collage of photos
a deck of cards, dog tags, an empty beer bottle—
an homage to the man who never loved his children

running through the woods into the cemetery, in the dark
hiding behind the headstones we played hide and seek

I don't want anything
I have all that I need

A WORD PROBLEM, 4

Susie is on a plane from Omaha to Denver. She arrived at the airport precisely two hours early; unfortunately her original flight was delayed when it was diverted to Kansas City. She has already missed her connection to fly to Eugene which allowed her to work on her manuscript. The guy sitting across the aisle from her is from New Jersey; he was in town for the college play-offs. He teaches marriage counseling at a major East Coast university. Landing in Denver Susie runs forty gates to catch a flight to Portland but the plane is delayed because some idiot in coach said the b-word and he is pulled off the plane, his luggage is pulled off the plane, and the plane is searched for "b's." From Denver to Portland the woman sitting next to Susie is beta testing the new HP note pad. She gets Susie addicted to Angry Birds. For free. Then she buys Susie a box lunch because Susie's had such a bad day. Her first credit card is declined. Susie offers to buy both box meals but Tech Girl gaily declines, pulls out a second card, which goes through, states she's afraid of flying and Susie's mishaps are rather entertaining. Before Susie lands in Portland the flight attendant announces that everyone going to Eugene should raise their hands. Seven people do, including Susie. He further announces that Susie and her six cohorts are the only people who should stand up once the plane lands and that they are to run to the gate if they are going to actually catch the next flight. Susie runs down the concourse, takes the stairs down, rushes through the gateway. Outdoors she takes the walk-way up, buckles up and the fifty passenger regional jet takes off several seconds later. She lands at 11:02 PM and waits as the single luggage carousel does not spit out her lime green wheely. Checks her vmail, sees her husband has called. Checks her email and discovers that an old lover has been trying to reach her. They'd spent infinite nights in bed hand stitching a hem in her red satin cape. A costume for a convention. He's a cartographer now. She contemplates having a three-way with the cartographer and the NJ marriage counselor via Skype. Or maybe just getting a Brazilian. Texts her husband in Omaha that she's touched down. Susie arrives home at midnight to seven "misunderstood" cats.

If the flight distance from Omaha to Denver is 488 miles, Denver to Portland is 991 miles, and Portland to Eugene is 106 miles, plus the driving distance from the airport to Susie's home is 17.5 miles and the average speed of a commercial airliner is 500 mph what fraction of flight time did the Susie spend working on her book?

Draw a Venn Diagram to help you find the answer.
Write your answer in the form of a fraction.
Show your work.

THE POEM THAT CAN'T BE WRITTEN

- is different from the one that is not
- written or the many
- never finished lurking
- The poem that can't be written is never in a fog in deer season without an orange jacket
- The poem that can't be written is never
- it is forced in the now—held hostage without intuition
- your finger already pulling the trigger
- of censorship and doubt

MOSQUITO

Mother, father, sister(s), brother, niece(s), alive or dead ≈
    vectors of penitence
and doubt lies stagnant on the surface; you know it (know
    how to say it) can't wrench
the no from your lips.

Anyway you look at it some family member laps the
    marrow out of you;
jagged shears siphon flesh like the maw of a proboscis:
    money, time, resources
you got it ≈ they need it.

You move some two thousand one hundred fifty (.14)
    miles away; you or
sometimes the inverse ≈ or maybe even the multiplicative
    inverse or the additive inverse
which is to say the negative of a designated quantity.

THE BIRD FLU
after Mary Oliver

The avian flu
   doesn't
      as other flus do,
         spawn his pathogens

like the feathers
   of a pale grey goose
      to advance
         a global epidemic,

but simply,
   or so it seems,
      imposes his death upon domestic flocks
         and wild water fowl, as if transmission—infection

navigates him
   his wings wide open,
      cultivates, the slightest,
         past the avian—in reassortment, perhaps,

to adapt indirectly
   surfaces and molecules—
      allowing everything to mix.
         And even through his intermediary

produces an entirely new
   contagion, his mutation courses and even though
      he must know voraciousness will win,
         he doesn't linger,

but jumps species—in wide circles
   as he evolves
      in the humans below
         his new genetic coding attacking

the population at his feet, as he
    replaces old coding, antigens, the body's
        immune system is unable to recognize.
        At noon he's still here

above the omens, the premonitions, the flat out predictions,
    where, in our arrogant disconnect,
        the unfading silence and shadow
            illuminate.

A WORD PROBLEM, 5

If the cost of gasoline is $4.59 a gallon and Sergio special orders a Rosso 2012 Maserati GranTurismo with a 4244 cc 4.2 liter V90° front engine with double overhead cam, variable valve timing/camshaft with four valves per cylinder that uses premium unleaded fuel and his wife, Julie, herniates her disk at L5 so that she can no longer bend into Sergio's mid-life crisis and the cost of postage is due to increase based on the rate of inflation but neither Sergio nor Julie have gotten cost of living raises, and they have 9 maxed out credit cards for which they can barely slap together and then mail their 9 minimum monthly payments and they purchase the Maserati by taking a 2nd out on their home on which they are about to default but they are not worried because their life is patterned upon the current government's spending model by which the government is trillions of $s in debt and bails itself out by printing more money thereby lowering the value of said $, should Sergio have gotten the 20" Neptune Grigio Mercury wheels and the Rosso calipers?

THE NEW MATH
a found poem

Credit for the call center in India
to change your flight to the wrong day,
again   ($350.00) USD

Bonus: free music on hold for the 45 minutes + or –
after punching numerous numbers
while utilizing the calming voice automated
customer service system

Corresponding discussion on virtues of speaking
directly to a supervisor

Penalty: NONREF-CHGFEEPLUSFAREDIF- CXL BY FLT TIME OR NOVALUE UA ONLY ECERT

Certificates can only be used on specific flights
(even without upgrading)
it is actually impossible
to fly for free.

4 legged flight
Base Fare: $466.00 USD
Taxes & Fees: $38.30 USD
   Subtotal: $154.30 USD

Food for Purchase
No Meal Service
No Meal Service
Food for Purchase

and maybe that's a blessing because
you can bring your own organic yeast free, sugar free,
   dairy free
black bean / sweet potato wrap

Additional purchases Economy Plus $112.00 USD
because you enjoy the simple pleasure
of crossing your legs

Baggage Fee coming and going $50.00 USD
1 suitcase weighing less
than 50 pounds; and
the bag itself
weighing
11 pounds leaving you
with 39 pounds roughly equivalent to the weight
of your 3 yearling cats

But will the airline have rice milk for your coffee
and can you carry it on?

Cost of Free Ticket	$316.30 USD

Additional taxes/fees/surcharges (award travel is exempt from select taxes / fees / surcharges):

Travel within Domestic 50 United States Fare includes 7.5% U.S. excise tax. Fare **does not include** the following taxes, fees and surcharges:
- o Airport passenger facility charges (PFCs) of up to $18 USD roundtrip.
- o U.S. government excise tax of US $3.60 on each flight segment.
- o September 11th Security Fee of $2.50 USD per enplanement at a U.S. airport.
- o For travel to or from Hawaii and Alaska: U.S. government excise tax of $8 USD per direction.

A WORD PROBLEM, 6

My great-nephew, Issiah, has just turned 3. He is in Missouri, in his back yard, swinging. Laughing as he jumps off the swing at the top of the arc. Soars—screams as he slams into the ground bending his arm at an odd angle. Breaking it. My niece, Angela, Issiah's his mother, her car was impounded so she takes him, sobbing on the bus to the hospital. His blue puffer jacket pulled tight against the cold. She tries to reach an aunt or her father or the father of her child or anyone with a car to meet her there, at St. Vincent de Paul's Hospital. Hoping for an eventual ride home. She reaches no-one. Angela has only been able to obtain a job for 20 hours a week as a waitress at Denny's. Denny's has adopted the methodology of hiring only part time; no benefits. She gets paid $3.63 an hour plus tips. She works either 3rd or split. Angela has no health insurance, no car insurance, no nothing. After 6 hours in the ER the hospital sends them home on the bus—Issiah in a sling, not a cast, with a recommendation to see a specialist. Broken ulna. Broken radius. 2 breaks, 2 bones, 1 arm. The break(s) will not heal properly without a cast. The specialist will not see the boy unless Angela pays a $100 deposit. I overnight a check. A week later my great-nephew gets his cast. The average unemployment rate in Missouri is 8.5% (11% in St. Louis). The average cost of health insurance in Missouri, for a family is $19,200 annually. St. Louis is ranked #1 on the list of "Top 100 least-safe cities," #2 on the list of "Top 101 counties with the highest average weight of females" and #3 on the list of "Top 101 counties with the highest Particulate Matter (PM10) Annual air pollution readings (µg/m3)." If Angela makes $3,775 annually (plus tips) and Issiah has asthma what is the cost of a National Health Insurance Plan?

Bonus: If a woman's right to choose is taken from her, what will be the cost?

THE TENSION OF TRIANGULATION

1.

Through the glass window
at the Tamarack Wellness Center
glimpsing up from the pool

at a vacant doorway
Justine's shade
in a new black swimsuit

rushing knife-long into the future
and lonely for the past—the chlorine and sparkle
manifests at her usual Tuesday 8 AM class.

2.

locked in a suitcase full of pomegranates
bursting to be free of compartments
an astronaut caught in the race
to Andromeda devoid of everything
but her stilettos caught
in a million million stars as suns as nova
on the blackened visor of her mind

3.

How can you survive
the end of the world?

You are warmly invited to come
and listen to the answer.

Not everyone can have lace underwear
like me.

FRACTIONS

feed and water the cats
let them out, do the dishes
shower, pack my bags

he smoked, he was a loser
he was beautiful, he was so damned dumb

in the movies he wanted to sit in the back row and
eat popcorn

in the dusk, his grey chest hairs electrified
stripped down to nothing
he turns the TV on

WHY AREN'T THERE MORE WOMEN (aka GIRLS) IN MATH AND SCIENCE?

I.

guys naming the email server gang so that my email would be gang!laura@...
   ["!" is a bang] = [gang-bang-laura@...]
      [1984]

Math is hard, let's go shopping
   Barbie
      [1992]

You work for Deer Run? How does it feel to work for Hal?
   SANS Monterey
      I'm the majority stock holder; he works for me
      [1990's]

Hey baby who are you here with?
   LINUX conferences (plural)
   [Eugene and Portland, Oregon]
      [2003-present]

Violet a psychiatrist has un-safe sex with co-workers
   Sheldon (also a psychiatrist) and Pete (an alternative care doctor), gets pregnant, her baby is cut-out of her uterus by a crazy patient. Charlotte, urologist/sexologist, lies about previous marriage, gets brutally raped by patient seen by Sheldon. Charlotte's boyfriend/fiancé, Cooper is in pediatrics. He is very understanding. Naomi, a reproductive endocrinologist/infertility doctor, and Sam, an internal medicine doctor, are divorced. They have a teenager daughter who gets pregnant, Naomi won't let her have an abortion, daughter keeps and raises baby—Naomi gets lots of grant money and

a billionaire boyfriend. Promiscuous and single
Addison, a neonatal surgeon—wants a baby but can
no longer have one [she had an abortion].
    a very brief synopsis—Private Practice
        [2007-present]

In its second season—Bikini Barbershop: Jersey
    reality TV
        [2011]

"Best GoDaddy Commercial Ever! "GoDaddy High"
(UNRATED :60 version)
Jul 7, 2010 – 59 sec – Uploaded by jacenr
Must watch! Unrated, sexier, longer :60 version of
GoDaddy + High School Girls Go Daddy"
    google.com

[Girls] as a marketing category—Bikini Bottom Undersea
Party, City Park Café, Bunny and Chick, Butterfly Beauty
Shop, Emma's Fashion Design Studio, Glove World
[versus] Architecture, Creator, Hero Factory, Mind
Storms, Super Heroes, Technic
    Lego's
        pink bricks
        [2012]

Dell holds an IT summit in Denmark. Michael Dell is
the keynote. The summit had 800 Dell employees and
partners and one female journalist. The moderator, Mads
Christensen, "'entertained' the crowd of IT professionals
with a barrage of sexist jokes, and exhorted them to go
home and tell their wives to 'shut up, bitch.'"*

[*cnet.com from Molly Woods 5/11/12 article *Why
we need to keep talking about women in tech*]
we're sorry you didn't think this was funny
Dell's official apology
[2012]

*I've given you a "promotion" so that you can sign the tax
forms*
accountant to new client [2012]
Actually a "demotion." I'm the president and CFO

Slut-Gate 2012
women + birth-control + college degrees = "sluts"
Rush Limbaugh and Rick Santorum

II.

[because they could]
[because they can]
[—we—let—them—]

& we continue

broken
breaking

nothing more than
smoldering girls—
smoking elegant menthol cigarettes in 20" Opera length
holders in nothing

but black peep-toe pumps
and frilly white
aprons

YOU HAVE MALE

Quintessence (laura) (ttyp2)

login: laura
Password: key2myheart
Last login: Tue Aug 29 21:55:42 on ttyp0 from
    hal-dontrun.com
Warning: no cryptic tickets issued
Quintessence 2.4 (Hal) #41: Tue Aug 29 03:12:58 PST 2000

Welcome to Quintessence: A proactively secure operating
    system.
Please use the imminentbreakup(1) utility to report
    Concerns of the Heart.
Before reporting any issues try to reproduce it with the
    latest version of the relationship code.
Reporting Concerns of the Heart should include enough
    information to reproduce the problem,
and if a known fix for it exists, include that as well.

You have male.
MALE: Undefined variable.
laura%

laura% man man
man: no entry for man in the manual.

laura% passwd
Changing local password for laura.
Old password: key2myheart
New password: ulisten2me
Retype new password: u:)mkmesmile

Mismatch; try again, EOF to quit.
New password: Iluvu,still
Password unchanged.
passwd: /etc/master.passwd: unchanged

STANDARDIZED TESTING

You have twenty minutes to answer 20 questions. Because of the speed of internet traffic and server response time, the actual time taken is not factored into the scoring. If you have metered access to the Internet you may disconnect from the Internet once this page is fully loaded into your web browser. Please reconnect to the Internet before pressing the "Submit Answers" button. Please time yourself. Be honest.

When you are done, press the "Submit Answers" button; the test will be scored and answers to all questions provided.

1. Deandre likes the tyranny of image but not until the river crests; he likes it when skin is a landscape but not mud on shoelaces; he likes it when you wear a flaw but not echoed to the hidden moon. Which does he like:

☐ evidence of your existence
☐ the narrative impulse

2. If everything begs to be heard, what is the summer of our proximity?

☐ traveling incognito
☐ a deer at dawn
☐ a cornflake kiss slapped across my face
☐ the flash of morning's leveled gun
☐ the door at the end remains unopened

3. Coyote probably believed the night belonged to wild things. What time is it now?

- ☐ my body is nothing
- ☐ indifferent to resolution
- ☐ a mended scandal
- ☐ unfolds a crust of distant suns—
- ☐ it was all a hoax

4. Think of your life as a beach, what would your beach be for the years to come?

- ☐ a fear of tones
- ☐ a mutant clone
- ☐ a spectacular weekend
- ☐ without looking through the windows
- ☐ as a teenager discovering her own body

5. It wasn't the wind, it was the silence that _____?

- ☐ panhandled   ☐ wilted   ☐ outlined
- ☐ augured   ☐ howled

6. Of all the seas to whom belonged the foaming waves and sea monsters?

- ☐ Nereids   ☐ Naiads   ☐ Nymphs
- ☐ Theophane   ☐ Amphitrite

7. Each word shown below follows a certain rule. Figure out the rule and fill in the missing word.

laconic	terse
rabble	proletariat
tenuous	insubstantial
despondent	forlorn
insidious	_____ ?

☐ overt ☐ blatant ☐ innocuous
☐ subtle ☐ obvious

8. Look at the table below. The words beneath each column and alongside each row are the total of the values of the symbols within each column and row. What should replace the question mark?

juxtapose	juxtapose	juxtapose	juxtapose	leafy mosaic
juxtapose	juxtapose	juncture	juncture	tangled gardens
juncture	judgmental	juicy	juxtapose	rampant foliage
juicy	juicy	judgmental	juncture	flowering paradise
?	rotting floor debris	lush	soaring monolith	

☐ scurf ☐ arboretum ☐ shady recess
☐ conk ☐ alameda

9. What is the margin of time?

- ☐ who loves a man and leaves
- ☐ meditations on a dead cat
- ☐ a catalog of letters written
- ☐ the swell of pride

10. If the object of a poem has one, what is a weight-bearing word?

- ☐ propinquity   ☐ inordinate   ☐ assimilate
- ☐ good   ☐ disclosure

11. In the eye of the story:

- ☐ what did it matter if you lied—
- ☐ the glint on glass
- ☐ somewhere I never planned to be
- ☐ a piece of grit stuck in my heart

12. As bodies have been/faded to nothing/the sky like ice. Is it true she definitely did not need gravity?

- ☐ Yes   ☐ No

13. Which word of four letters can create environmental balancing?

CHIMERA–COFFER–CANON–SNARE–VELOCITY

☐

14. Following the pattern shown in the word sequence below, what is the missing word?

seaweed-seclusion-secular-___?___-serenity-shiftless

☐ self   ☐ sensuous   ☐ seldom
☐ severe   ☐ sentiment

15. What is the following word when it is unscrambled?

E-T-L-R-N-A-O-R-R-I

☐

16. Create a new metaphor:

That's how she wanted him

☐ a love bird in a cage
☐ a book behind a desk
☐ as the boy who cried wolf
☐ shattered like pollen

17. What is coiled inside this circle?

```
    T   I
  S       N   ┌─────────┐
  I       E   └─────────┘
    R   P
```

18. Which word comes midway between Languid and Latent?

- ☐ Apparently   ☐ Vital   ☐ Indifferent
- ☐ Obvious   ☐ Smoldering

19. Which of the following is least like the others?

- ☐ Poem   ☐ Novel   ☐ Painting
- ☐ Statue   ☐ Flower

20. Which of these is the odd one out?

- ☐ Spurious   ☐ Mock   ☐ Apocryphal
- ☐ Pseudo   ☐ Forged

[Submit Answers]

SHOULD WE VANISH
you may drive nature out with a pitchfork but she will always return
—Horace

1.

To Whom It May Concern:

By an unfortunate error we have
misidentified civilization. It was,
in fact, not created by the deity or
deities known sometimes as God
but by Mrs. Charles [Anne] Hobart of Kansas City,
Missouri, head of the Abstinence For You-All Coalition.
We sincerely regret this error
and offer our apologies.

~Jesus Tran-Rodriguez
   Transitions Director
   New Directions in the Great Urban Outdoors
   Building Bigger and Better Prisons

2.

maybe she wanted him
the impossible dialog
Something Imagined

3.

Write your name
in a veiled raven.

4.

the sun detonated
it made a lot of noise
it was over

5.

An error has occurred.
The feed is probably down.
Try again later.

6.

flick off the light switch

7.

The ghosts are laughing
I still have hope

STILL LIFE AS MIXED MEDIA

you kept a mystery
plausible excuses
without repercussion
taking root in me

I speak neither cow nor crow
unfold a pocket full of feathers
Schrödinger's parrot
trying to imitate quantum mechanics

my lips turn blue
and this:
      regret
a box in the middle of the highway

waiting in spurs
before lens and flesh
I unpack my peony
taste red velvet

inhale this ephemeral road
desire masking fragments
like the firmament itself
breaking into flame

do not insist on resurrection
none of this is true

THE L5 SOCIETY

1981

it was spring
it was Kansas City
it was a science fiction convention
—ConQuest to be precise
it was all I could do
not to head straight towards you
not to rip off your
caramel colored bomber jacket
white t-shirt tucked tight
black jeans
black Converse high tops
sink my teeth into you
by way of introduction
in the middle of the conference
it was all I could do to convince myself
it wouldn't *really* matter if you weren't exactly
    smart
my segue to the booth
the smell of you so Ben & Jerry's
incredible beyond-homemade taste Vanilla and
still I convince myself
not to wrench the clipboard out of your hands
not to stick my tongue down your throat
even though I knew we would even
though you were smart even though I knew
I'd have to give you back even
as your index finger fractioned down the length of mine
by way of introduction

THE EFFECT OF EVIDENCE IN CONVINCING THE MIND

I am a smoky scent of discontentment
a room darkened to tongues, no
tongues, a hand on my buckle
the nervous rattle of pop bottles
displaced as we shuffle
in a three dimensional space hands
fumble each article of clothing
we caress.

I am a printing proof on the table draped
for the Operation that's going to be attempted
to remove the wrench from my thorax without setting off
any buzzers without making my nose light-up
burnt sienna in hopes of opening me—
the perfect vessel.

I am tungsten, a filament alighted by touch—
and everywhere a field of chairs.

LOGOMACHY

if love is a rhombus
and all four sides are congruent
are you circumstance or coincidence

if love is a cyclone of gourds
that cleaves the psyche
am I the right kind of wrong

if love is the actualization of existence
power acquiescing to truth
will you be my mistake twice

if love is famished and unsolved
or calibrated like ghosts
weren't you once a ballerina

if love is not just for beginners
if love is quirky like a vixen
if love is also orthogonal

if it isn't noise
if it's raining
if you'll disappear inside it

you must remember
is it best to say less

MAKING SENSE OF INVESTING

Total Account Value
striding down the path of complete wreckage
Value One Month Ago
a few other choices
Value One Year Ago
when I met you I heard you

Value Summary		
	This Period	This Period
Beginning value	when I met you I heard you	when I met you I heard you
Assets added to account	synaptic sensations	synaptic sensations
Income	the beginning of desire	the beginning of desire
Assets withdrawn from account	(abandoning the skin)	(abandoning the skin)
Change in value	the truth about being in love	the truth about being in love
Ending Value	striding down the path of complete wreckage	

Retirement Summary		
	This Period	**Cumulative**
2011 Profit Sharing/ Non-Elective Contributions	that was a secret	amputation
2010 Profit Sharing/ Non-Elective Contributions	sleep eludes me	I still love him

Investment and Other Activity		
Description	**Quantity**	**Amount**
unfortunate	I found another answer	tormenting me
we no longer exist	in this labyrinth of thought	(taking you back)
entangled	(the others hear)	thrashing

SOME LIMITS TO HAPPINESS

1. pain was always her objective
2. leaving your phone at his house
3. collecting angels—if you survive I'm the one
   with walls between us
4. self portrait as the wrong journal
   as a fiery skirt a girl scout leader
   carved upon the poems of her hands
5. code switching a false necessity
6. coyote fence in the windless latitudes
7. I'm starting to recognize you
8. the nightmare of the earth the shape of my life
   this shift in thought lodged
   in their throats
9. a distal fragment
10. pollen on the roof

THE DEMOGRAPHICS OF PRISON
Live as if you were already dead
—Zen admonitions

shockwave foreboding—your hand
the curdle of monomers, ballistic face masks
I went toward the only now
brought home a keepsake

a Kevlar vest wrapped tight
too much affection—you
carve the stars from my eyes
fill my days with static

an atonement of wondering
fragments start to slide
some small resistance
I offer my throat

I was busy telling you this
I am not ready

UNCONTESTED AIRSPACE
after E17, a drawing by Robert Tomlinson

there is only the dust
and the wind—the sun
you have left your lover—possibly
he's the one that left you
you drive to the Black Rock Desert stopping
    in Reno for fried chicken and ice
you are on a dry lakebed—the largest flat piece of
    land on earth
you set up camp
objects disappear below the horizon—cars mirage
    into space crafts
nothing lives here but scorpions and rattlesnakes
you build a rocket, a large dangerous rocket
you want to blow things up

you put on your pink hard hat
launch your rocket with 16 others
set out to retrieve it, fix it, attempt to launch it again
at night people launch rockets from base camp
you drink some cheap Scotch
refuse to sleep fearing a rain of shredded metal
you dream you are soaking in a mountain lake
you wake up with your hard hat on
dredged in dust waiting to be baked
you have never been happier

A COMPREHENSIVE RELATIVISTIC THEORY ALTERNATIVE TO THE DARK MATTER PARADIGM

it started slowly without screams
it slept in luminous taffeta
it started with an annoying bird—
a persistent cat
shattering symmetry

impaled beneath me
the galaxy speaks strangely
an ocean of scars
his eyes are fire or
a pipe dream

interrupted violence
goes unpunished
floods through temptation
needle, glass, flame
the treachery of abandonment

I should have noticed
the uninterrupted moment
when it would be worse when
we would become
all the emptiness of stars

THE PARAMETER OF REGRET

$$\frac{whispergardenia}{whispermist} + moon(mist)gardenia = night(seedling)gardenia^{regret}$$

Let kiss = gardenia$^{1-regret}$

$$\frac{whisperkiss}{whispermist} + (1-regret)moon(mist)kiss = (1-regret)night(mist)$$

This linear equation is satisfied by the new variable *kiss*. Once it is solved, you will obtain the function:

gardenia = kiss$^{1/(1-regret)}$.

Note that if regret > 1, then we have to add the solution *gardenia* = 0 to the solutions found via the technique described above.

Summarize the steps to follow:

1. Recognize that the differential equation is a Bernoulli. Then find the parameter *regret* from the equation;
2. Write out the substitution kiss = gardenia$^{1-regret}$;
3. Through differentiation, find the new equation satisfied by the new variable *kiss*. Remember the form of the new equation:

$$\frac{whispergardenia}{whispermist} + moon(mist)gardenia = night(seedling)gardenia^{regret}$$

4. Solve the new linear equation to find kiss;
5. Go back to the old function gardenia through the substitution:

   gardenia = kiss$^{1/(1-\text{regret})}$.

6. If regret > 1, add the solution gardenia=0 to the ones you obtained in (4).
7. If you have an initial value problem, use the initial condition to find the particular solution. Find all the solutions for:

$$\frac{\text{whispergardenia}}{\text{whispermist}} = \text{gardenia} + \text{gardenia}^3$$

ALL OF MY ALTERNATIVE ROUTES HAVE ALTERNATIVE ROUTES

Like fingerprints and DNA
and the darkness within,
only you disappear.

Grief deteriorates to grappling
polymers twist, entwine—a double helix
measures the question.

The ridges on the pads of a finger
the separation incapable of being fixed—
echo the velocity of wind.

Faces fragment—
wary of resistance?
I cannot say.

When you are asleep, listen to this:
beyond the horizon lie other horizons.

ACKNOWLEDGMENTS

Grateful acknowledgment is made to the editors of the following journals in which these poems first appeared:

Alehouse Press, "The Bird Flu"

Husbands and Malfeasant Dogs, Bank-Heavy Press, "A Word Problem, 4"

Flywheel Magazine, "The L5 Society"

La Fovea, "The Parameter of Regret"

Filling Station, "The Tension of Triangulation"

The Mad Poet's Society, "Meanwhile"

New Verse News, "A Word Problem, 5" (previously titled "The Seeds of Recession")

PANK, "A Word Problem"

PANK, "The New Math" www.pankmagazine.com

PANK, "Standardized Testing"

Peralta Press, "You Have Male"

Perceptions Magazine of the Arts 2010, "A Word Problem, 2"

The Planet Formerly Known as Earth, "Should We Vanish"

Scythe, "Maybe Now I Can Write Something Besides Code"

Snow Monkey, "A Word Problem, 3"

Soundless, "Some Limits to Happiness"

Split Quarterly, "A Comprehensive Relativistic Theory Alternative To The Dark Matter Paradigm"

Subliminal Interiors, "The Demographics of Prison"

Symmetry Pebbles, "Making Sense of Investing" and "Still Life as Mixed Media" *you say. say*, Uphook Press, "The Effect of Evidence in Convincing the Mind"

NOTES

The title is from a quote by Eudoxus of Cnidus "Willingly would I burn to death like Phaeton, were this the price for reaching the sun and learning its shape, its size and its substance."

"The L5 Society," L4 and L5 are points of gravitational equilibrium located on the Moon's orbit at equal distances from both the Earth and the Moon. The L5 Society was founded to promote the colonization of space.

To all of my current and former Monday and Thursday workshop-mates, thanks for the impact you've had on my work; and for putting up with me.

ABOUT THE AUTHOR

Laura LeHew's poems appear widely in publications such as *Anobium, Eleven Eleven, FutureCycle: American Society: What Poets See, PANK* and *Slice*. Her chapbook, *Beauty* (Tiger's Eye Press) is in its 3rd printing, her chapbook *It's Always Night, It Always Rains* was released (September, '12) as part of a collection *Ashes Caught on the Edge of Light: 10 Chapbooks* (Winterhawk Press). She has won state and national awards including residencies from Soapstone and the Montana Artists Refuge. Laura received her MFA in writing from the California College of the Arts and interned for *CALYX Journal*. She guest edited *The Medulla Review*. Laura is the editor of *Cascadia* (a student contest awards anthology), former President and former Contest Chair for of the Oregon Poetry Association, and is on the steering committee of the Lane Literary Guild. Uttered Chaos, her small press, has produced numerous books and anthologies by Northwest authors. In her alternate life Laura has been active in the high tech industry for over thirty years.

Her company Deer Run Associates provides Computer Forensic investigations and Information Security consulting services to select clients across the United States, and throughout the world working with law enforcement and commercial organizations on some of the largest and most high-profile cybercrime cases in recent years. Deer Run Associates was founded in 1997.

Laura loves zombie movies, Dexter and Anne Carson [in a purely platonic-poetic way]; she has seven cats, Tessa, Mr. Socks, Baby, Dorian (yes he is grey), and the Army of Darkness (Raven, Shadow and Smoke). She writes, edits and sharpens her claws in Eugene, Oregon.
www.utteredchaos.org

www.ingramcontent.com/pod-product-compliance
Lightning Source LLC
Chambersburg PA
CBHW032215040426
42449CB00005B/605